HAL•LEONARD
INSTRUMENTAL
PLAY-ALONG

AUDIO
ACCESS
INCLUDED

PLAYBACK+
Speed • Pitch • Balance • Loop

TRUMPET

IRISH FAVORITES

CONTENTS

Title	Page	Title	Page
Believe Me, If All Those Endearing Young Charms	2	The Jolly Beggarman	17
The Bells of St. Mary's	3	The Little Beggarman	18
Black Velvet Band	4	MacNamara's Band	19
Brennan on the Moor	5	Minstrel Boy	20
Cockles and Mussels	6	My Wild Irish Rose	21
The Croppy Boy	7	A Nation Once Again	22
Danny Boy	8	The Old Orange Flute	23
Easy and Slow	9	The Patriot Game	24
The Foggy Dew	10	Red Is the Rose	25
Green Grow the Rushes, O	11	The Rising of the Moon	26
The Humour Is on Me Now	12	The Rose of Tralee	27
I Once Loved a Lass	13	Too-Ra-Loo-Ra-Loo-Ral	28
I'll Take You Home Again, Kathleen	14	The Wearing of the Green	29
I'll Tell Me Ma	15	When Irish Eyes Are Smiling	30
The Irish Rover	16	The Wild Colonial Boy	31
		Wild Rover	32

To access audio visit:
www.halleonard.com/mylibrary

Enter Code
1904-2316-4262-1221

ISBN 978-1-4234-9528-4

HAL•LEONARD®
CORPORATION
7777 W. BLUEMOUND RD. P.O. BOX 13819 MILWAUKEE, WI 53213

Visit Hal Leonard Online at
www.halleonard.com

BELIEVE ME, IF ALL THOSE ENDEARING YOUNG CHARMS

TRUMPET

Words and Music by
THOMAS MOORE

THE BELLS OF ST. MARY'S

TRUMPET

Words by DOUGLAS FURBER
Music by A. EMMETT ADAMS

BLACK VELVET BAND

TRUMPET

Traditional

BRENNAN ON THE MOOR

TRUMPET

Traditional

COCKLES AND MUSSELS
(Molly Malone)

TRUMPET

Traditional

THE CROPPY BOY

TRUMPET

18th Century Irish Folksong

DANNY BOY

TRUMPET

Words by FREDERICK EDWARD WEATHERLY
Traditional Irish Folk Melody

EASY AND SLOW

TRUMPET

Traditional

THE FOGGY DEW

TRUMPET

Traditional

GREEN GROW THE RUSHES, O

TRUMPET

Traditional

THE HUMOUR IS ON ME NOW

TRUMPET

Traditional

I ONCE LOVED A LASS

TRUMPET

Traditional

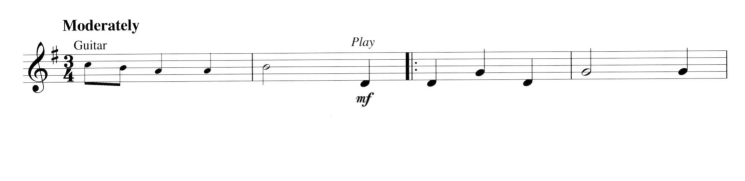

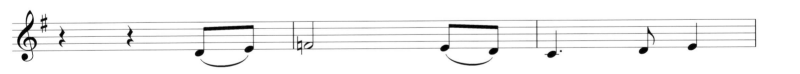

I'LL TAKE YOU HOME AGAIN, KATHLEEN

TRUMPET

Words and Music by
THOMAS WESTENDORF

I'LL TELL ME MA

TRUMPET

Traditional

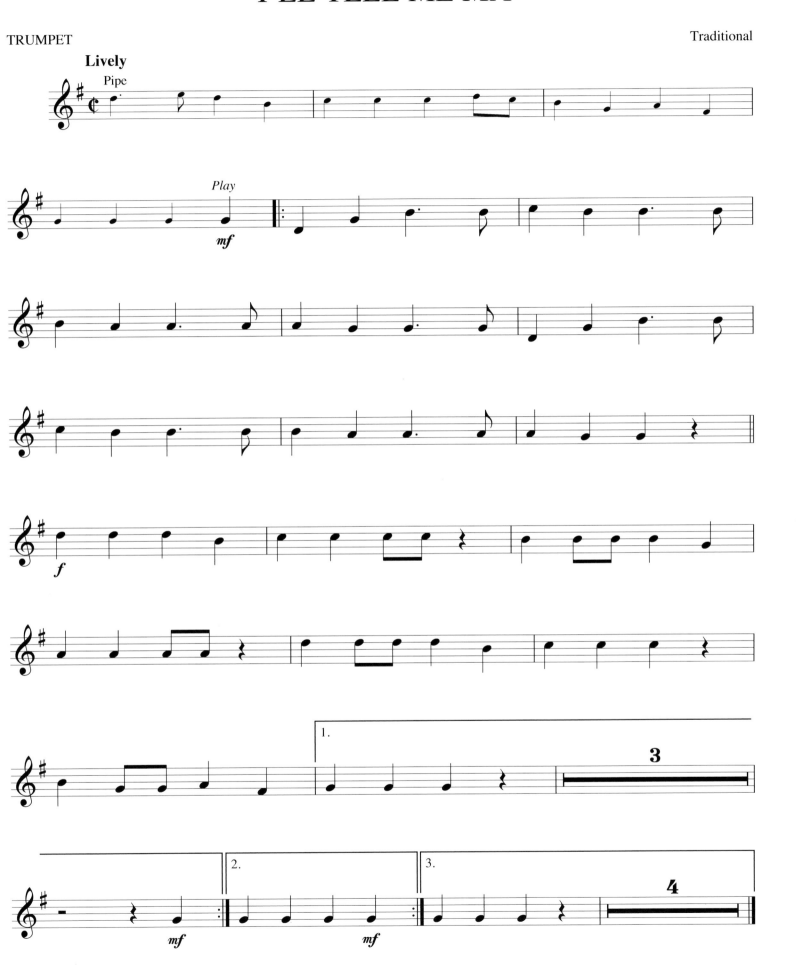

THE IRISH ROVER

TRUMPET

Traditional

THE JOLLY BEGGARMAN

TRUMPET

Traditional

THE LITTLE BEGGARMAN

TRUMPET

Traditional

MacNAMARA'S BAND

TRUMPET

Words by JOHN J. STAMFORD
Music by SHAMUS O'CONNOR

Lively March

MINSTREL BOY

TRUMPET

Traditional

MY WILD IRISH ROSE

TRUMPET

Words and Music by
CHAUNCEY OLCOTT

A NATION ONCE AGAIN

TRUMPET

Words and Music by
THOMAS DAVIS

THE OLD ORANGE FLUTE

TRUMPET

Traditional

THE PATRIOT GAME

TRUMPET

Traditional

RED IS THE ROSE

TRUMPET

Irish Folksong

THE RISING OF THE MOON

TRUMPET

Traditional

THE ROSE OF TRALEE

TRUMPET

Words by C. MORDAUNT SPENCER
Music by CHARLES W. GLOVER

TOO-RA-LOO-RA-LOO-RAL
(That's an Irish Lullabye)

TRUMPET

Words and Music by
JAMES R. SHANNON

THE WEARING OF THE GREEN

TRUMPET

18th Century Irish Folksong

WHEN IRISH EYES ARE SMILING

TRUMPET

Words by CHAUNCEY OLCOTT
and GEORGE GRAFF, JR.
Music by ERNEST R. BALL

THE WILD COLONIAL BOY

TRUMPET

Traditional

WILD ROVER

TRUMPET

Traditional